STEADFAST!

Fifty-one Missions in a B-24 Liberator

By Robert J. Lick

Consolidated Publishing

Oviedo, Lucca, Nara, Boise

B-24 Waist Gunner

Dedication

For My Crew Members

William L. Donald, Pilot
Allen J. Smith, Co-Pilot
Stuart J. Lefkowits, Navigator
Everett A.G. Lorenz, Bombardier
John R. Walling, Flight Engineer
Angelo Marino, Radio Operator
Cleo H. West, Nose Turret Gunner
Ernest Balint, Ball Turret Gunner
Vernon T. Miller, Tail Gunner

From
Robert J. Lick, Waist Gunner

Introduction

I've produced over a dozen books about the careers of World War II veterans, starting with a summary of my father-in-law's wartime experiences, which began in the Aleutian Islands and then progressed through the Pacific, all the way to Okinawa. Eventually, I created other books covering the war in both Europe and the Pacific and nearly every branch of the service. Later, I compiled all of these stories into some publications which are annotated at the end of this book. I always relished the opportunity to create these memorials for our veterans and their families and friends. Besides the precious memories that are captured and shared, I am rewarded by learning about whole realms of history which were nothing but a mystery before.

The subject of this book, Robert J. Lick, came to my attention when a high school friend, Karen Drysdale Phillips, mentioned on FaceBook that she met Bob at an animal therapy farm where she volunteers. I followed up and contacted Bob's daughter, Laura, and she arranged interviews with Bob. She also provided family photographs, which are incorporated into this book. Her sister, Lisa, also collected information from Bob and passed it on to me. In all of this work I tried to capture Bob's thoughts and his way of speaking, and make sure that this book has his full approval.

Bob Lick and Karen Drysdale Phillips at SOUL Harbour Ranch, Barrington, Illinois

This introductory section is a good place to mention Bob's place in the successful campaigns to liberate Europe. He was a waist gunner in a B-24, a strategic bomber known as "The Liberator," which flew out of Manduria, Italy, in the middle of the stiletto heel of the Italian boot in the region called Puglia.

The Italian Boot, with Manduria in the Center

Bob was part of the 15th Air Force and its subsidiary 47th Bomb Wing. The 15th Air Force was responsible for the Mediterranean, Eastern Europe, Austria, and Southern Germany. It was composed of tens of thousands of airmen and thousands of planes.

15th Air Force Embroidered Patch

47th Bomb Wing Insignia

Within the 47th Bomb Wing, there were several bomb groups. Bob was assigned to the 450th Bomb Group, and within that group, Bob was part of the 722nd Bomb Squadron.

450th Bomb Group,
("The Cottontails"), Leather Patch

722nd Bomb Squadron,
"Holy Joe" Patch

Bob enlisted in the Army just after his birthday in November, 1942, when he was 20 years old, and trained for almost two years before flying across the Atlantic to join his squadron in Italy. There he served for almost 8 months, logging 51 missions. He was on his way back home by May, 1945 and finally released from the service in October, almost three years after he first signed up.

After the war, Bob finished up his college degree, met and married Dorothy, the love of his life, raised four kids, and developed a successful career in the publishing business. He currently lives in North Barrington, Illinois and just turned 101.

Rich O'Hara
Boise, Idaho, November 23, 2023

STEADFAST!

Fifty-one Missions in a B-24 Liberator
By Robert J. Lick

Edited by Richard O'Hara

Cataloging in Publication Data:

Robert J. Lick (1922-)

World History

World War II

European Theater of Operations

Strategic Bombing Campaigns

1944 – 1945

15th Air Force

Recollections of Robert J. Lick, T/Sgt,
Serial # 17 039 164, U.S. Army Air Corps

Cover: Bob Lick in Front of a B-24

Frontispiece: B-24 Waist Gunner

Consolidated Publishing

Oviedo, Lucca, Nara, Boise

ISBN: 9798870755281
Printed in the USA

FIRST EDITION

STEADFAST!

Fifty-one Missions in a B-24 Liberator

By Robert J. Lick

CHAPTER ONE -- The Days of My Youth

I was born on November 23, 1922 in Richland, Missouri, the first child of Joseph and Lois Lick. We left soon after, when I was just a babe in arms, for Lebanon, Missouri, and then moved to Springfield, Chaffee, and Cape Girardeau. You see my Dad was a telegrapher on the St. Louis and San Francisco Railroad, the good old "Frisco" line. In those days a telegrapher who had seniority could take over the job of a junior employee whenever they wanted, so Dad was getting "bumped" every few years, and away we'd go to another town. That went on until after the Great Depression when Dad finally got promoted into a job that was exempt from this rule.

Frisco Line Telegrapher, 1941

Frisco Railroad Patch

I went to grade school in Lebanon, to middle school in Springfield, and to high school in Chaffee. In Lebanon we lived at 428 Jefferson Street in a house that rented for $25 per month. Mom and Dad were nearly the same age, Mom was born in 1897 and Dad in 1898. They were both Missouri natives. My sister, Helen, was born in 1927 when I was five.

Bob Lick, Wearing Short Pants, c. 1927

Lebanon Grade School on the Left and High School on the Right

We next headed off for Springfield, Missouri, where I attended Pipkin Middle School on Boonville Avenue.

Pipkin Middle School, Springfield, Missouri

The Frisco Lines had a large office in Springfield with a train engine out front.

Frisco Lines Office, Springfield, Missouri

I went to high school in Chaffee, Missouri and graduated in 1940. We were living at the time at 330 Davidson Avenue, in a rented house which cost my parents $35 a month. That would be about $800 a month in today's dollars. Dad was a trainmaster at the time and making $3,800 a year, so we were pretty well off. That's a salary of almost $80,000 in today's dollars. The Frisco Line had a large railyard in Chaffee, so that's where my Dad would have been spending his time.

Railyard, Chaffee, Missouri

My Grandpa was born in Illinois and he was a farmer in Lebanon and had three sons. When he passed away, Grandma sold the farm and moved into town. One of her sons, my uncle Bob Conner, was the fellow who taught me how to drive. Dad drove a Pontiac in those days, and that was our family car.

1938 Pontiac

After I graduated from high school, I enrolled at Drury College in Springfield. I guess you could say I was just taking a general course of education. Drury College was established in 1873 by Congregationalist home missionaries, patterned after the Congregationalist liberal arts colleges of the North, such as Oberlin, Dartmouth, Yale, and Harvard. We had quite a number of pre-med students attending there. We also had a chapel on campus called Stone Chapel, and weekly attendance was encouraged though not required.

Oddly enough, my aunt had gone to Drury 30 years before. She got her degree and worked as a missionary in Mexico for some time until she had some health problem and came back to be a school teacher in the southern part of the state. She never married. She was a subscriber to "The New York Times," probably one of about a half dozen subscriptions in the whole state. Aunt Edna was part of a Christian church in Springfield and the last time I was there they had a commemorative plaque on display mentioning her missionary work.

Drury College, Chapel

I was there in 1941 when Pearl Harbor was attacked. I was living in the Lambda Chi Alpha fraternity house at the time. I remember it was Sunday afternoon and I was listening to classical music on the radio. The broadcast was suddenly interrupted and I heard that the Japanese had attacked Hawaii. Everyone's immediate reaction was that we would have to sign up to fight. We naturally assumed we would be drafted or in the service soon. We would have to go, there was no question. We all listened to

FDR the next day when he addressed Congress. Most students did; there were about 400 of us at the time. We started taking more military courses after that.

After 2 ½ years of college I decided to enlist in the Air Corps reserves, hoping to become a pilot. I was young and handsome and figured I'd fit right in. I enlisted on November 26, 1942, right after my birthday. While I was awaiting orders to report for duty, I didn't return to Drury College, opting instead to enroll in Southeast Missouri State Teacher's College in Cape Girardeau and spend time with my family.

Southeast Missouri State

Without knowing it, this decision also allowed me to spend time with my mother, Lois, during the last few months of her life. Coincidentally, I got my orders to report for active duty on the day my mother died. After her funeral, I left for Jefferson Barracks in Lemay, Missouri, arriving on February 2, 1943, probably taking the old Frisco Line to get there. I was just 20 years old then.

Lois (Conner) Lick, c. 1935

Lois Lick, c. 1940

CHAPTER TWO -- Army Training

I no sooner got to Jefferson Barracks than they shipped me off after five weeks to a College Training Detachment at Coe College in Cedar Rapids, Iowa. I was in the first aircrew college training program up there. The Air Corps had a lot more volunteers than they needed, so they created a short-term training program that consisted of college courses in physics, math, history, geography, English, physical training, and military drill.[1]

College Training Detachment, Orientation Class
Water-Cooled .30 Calibre Machine Gun

---

[1] According to the Coe College webpage, by the end of 1942 93,000 men found themselves awaiting Air Corps training. The Army Air Force proposed to the War Department that the men be called to active duty and given a period of college training to make up educational shortcomings. In January 1943 the Secretary of War ordered the recommendations put into effect. Under contract with the Army, Coe College furnished room and board, limited medical services, along with physical training, and academic instruction. The first class came to Coe on March 1, 1943 (the group I was in). Classes, taught by college faculty, met on a regular schedule Monday through Friday. Instruction seldom proceeded in an orderly fashion. In addition to the regular nine hours per day of classes, the Army also required one hour per day of supervised study, one hour per day of physical training, and one hour per day of military drill. It was often a problem finding enough hours in the day for everything. Adding to the difficulties was the constant flow of men in and out of the Detachment.

Coe College, Library, Cedar Rapids, Iowa

Coe College, Science Hall

After 2 ½ months of the Coe College school, I was sent to Santa Ana Army Airbase in California for reassignment for further training. They quickly figured out that I didn't have perfect vision and couldn't go into pilot training. So, I was sent to training schools at Camp Kohler and Camp Pinedale in California. I wasn't in the Air Corps anymore at that point; I was actually attached to the Army Signal Corps. At Pinedale they were training signal technicians and I think they were aiming to send me to the Pacific to be an Army radio operator. I was not interested in doing that.

Signal Corps Training, Bob Lick (Right) Operating the Power Generator, c. 1943

I may have short circuited those plans to send me to the Pacific because I remember that I had this method for gumming up the works. I would approach the company clerk wherever I was assigned and ask if he could use the services of a good typist. That's like asking, "Would you like some chocolate cake?" The answer was always "Yes!" They were swamped with paperwork, so I'd start spending time in the office proving my worth. Eventually they wanted me full time, and I'd also mention a buddy of mine who was a natural comedian and great to have around. We'd both get transferred into that unit, but eventually the Army would catch up with us and get us out of there and back into our scheduled training. I believe I went to gunnery school in Yuma, Arizona, after the California schools. It was warm down there even though it was Christmas.

When all was said and done, after a year and a half of training, I was a radio operator and gunner qualified to join a B-24 crew training program at Davis Monthan Airbase in Tucson, Arizona. Somewhere along the line, probably at Yuma, I had also qualified with the M-1 carbine. Here's the medal they issue to show that you are carbine qualified.

Carbine Qualification Hanger

M-1 Carbine

Yuma Army Air Field (YAAF), Painted Leather Patch

I did pretty well at Air Corps gunnery school. They taught us how to shoot at moving targets because we were always going to be moving through the air, and so were the planes attacking us. We piled into Army trucks with shotguns and rode along and shot at targets. Some of the guys weren't familiar with shotguns and didn't hold it tight to their shoulder. The recoil caused a lot of bruises, so they looked for different solutions, including bringing their pillows with them. One time I scored 18 out of 20 hits. A lot of gunners could hardly hit one, but I had an instinct for leading a target just right. Maybe I inherited that instinct from my Dad. He was a good shot and he'd hunt quail when I was younger. We had a pointer named Queen who went with us.

At gunnery school they also taught us that a fighter plane is likely to attack from the rear along a pursuit course that allows him to overcome our airplane. Usually, they were approaching at an effective speed of about 100 miles per hour. However, our bullets were traveling about 200 mph in a forward direction, the same speed as our plane. So, we didn't lead the target. We were taught to shoot between the fighter plane and our tail and let our bullets catch up with it. The idea was to just fire a short burst behind the attacker's actual flight path, hoping the pursuing plane would fly into those bullets. They only had three seconds to fire at us, and we had three seconds to fire at them. We could fire about three dozen bullets in that time. Our waist guns were hand controlled so we didn't have the motorized turrets that were used in the nose, belly, and tail. This made it a bit harder to aim.

B-24 Waist Gunner, Publicity Picture

Our bomb crew training was in Tucson at Davis Monthan Airbase. That's where I met my crew members, and we trained together for several months learning how to fly the plane and carry out our bombing missions. It must have been the summer of 1944, and it was 100 degrees.

We would be heading off for a training flight, completely insulated and lugging all of our gear across the tarmac, including those heavy sheepskin jackets we needed to keep from freezing at altitude. That shearling was useless on the ground but much appreciated when we were flying in 40 below temperatures.

Here's our whole crew on the tarmac at Davis Monthan.

William A. Donald Crew, Davis Monthan AFB, Tucson, Arizona, Summer, 1944

Top Row, left to right: Navigator, Stuart J. Lefkowits; Co-pilot, Allen J. Smith; Pilot, William A. Donald; Bombardier, Everett A.G. Lorenz

Bottom Row, left to right: Flight Engineer, John R. Walling; Radio Operator, Angelo Marino; Nose Turret Gunner, Cleo H. West; Ball Turret Gunner, Ernest Balint; Tail Gunner, Vernon T. Miller; Waist Gunner, Robert J. Lick.

CHAPTER THREE -- The Flight to Italy

After our crew training was completed, we received secret orders to fly a new B-24 across the Atlantic to Italy. The plane was called the "Tulsamerican," and was a war bond plane. People of Tulsa, Oklahoma donated money to build the plane so they were allowed to name it and also to write their names on the fuselage. As far as I know it was common for newly trained crews to fly fresh airplanes to Europe. We weren't a special crew at all. However, many planes also arrived by ship. It depends on who you ask, because there were different experiences and impressions about that. We thought the Tulsamerican would be our plane once we arrived in Europe, but that airplane was the first thing the Air Corps took away from us when we arrived.

We first departed Wichita on September 18, 1944, after we did some test flights to acquaint ourselves with the plane. The first leg was from Wichita to Grenier Field in Manchester, New Hampshire. That's about 1,600 miles on a straight shot, or let's say an eight hour flight. This didn't bother us much because we had solid ground under us and plenty of places to land in case of an emergency. When we finally left, we flew to Italy together with several other planes, and we all attended the same briefing for each leg of the flight. We didn't fly in formation. We just took off and landed at about the same time.

Grenier Field, New Hampshire, c. 1941

We had lots of bad weather and it started in New Hampshire. We were headed overseas so for the first time I had to figure out what I was going to do with all my U.S. money because you couldn't spend it in Europe. It was time to drink up all I had, and I did my best. The next day's flight was cancelled due to bad weather, so what was I going to do now that I was out of money? Fortunately, I had a check book and could get some cash on base. Another night and another canceled flight and so on. It took me a while, but I finally ran out of money.

On the first clear day, we flew 2,350 miles from New Hampshire to the Azores. Figure ten hours plus for that journey. We sweated that one out; all that water.

The next destination was Marrakech, which is only a thousand mile flight, and then we took a small hop to Tunis (1,100 miles) and the final stretch was into Gioia, Italy, which was only 400 miles. We arrived on October 6, 1944, so we used up almost three weeks flying from Wichita to Gioia. I don't recall any complaints from the pilots and crew about the performance of the airplane enroute to Italy.

Sometimes we stayed more than one night after we landed. We assumed that after a long flight, such as New Hampshire to the Azores that we would have more than one night to recuperate, but we never knew for sure what would happen.

View of an Old Mosque

We were sent down to Lecce, Italy after we landed in Gioia and kept there for a few days while the Air Corps decided what to do with us. That's how we wound up in Manduria, Italy, right on the heel of the Italian peninsula, at an old aerodrome.

Lecce, Italy, Piazza del Duomo at Dawn

Roman Theatre, Lecce.

After we reached Italy, we were immediately consumed with preparations for combat missions, and we never really had a chance to reflect on our flight across the Atlantic or talk to each other about it. We just didn't have time.

Tulsamerican Crew, Arriving in Italy, October, 1944

Top Row: left to right: Stuart Lefkowits, Allen Smith,
Colonel Scott (Commanding Officer at Gioia and Tulsa Native),
William Donald, Everrett Lorenz

Bottom Row: left to right: Vernon Miller, Cleo West, Robert Lick,
Angelo Marino, John Walling, (Missing, Ernest Balint)

CHAPTER FOUR -- Air Combat Missions

Besides dropping bombs, our main role on the plane was to search for incoming fighters and repulse them. We couldn't do anything about the flak guns[2], but fighters were vulnerable to our .50 calibre machine guns. We rarely saw fighters except as we neared the target and as we left. They would show up to try to disrupt our bomb run and then chase after us when we were all trying to head home. Since our planes were manned by gunners who knew their business, we were an effective deterrent.

We were lucky to arrive in Italy when we did because a little before we got there, the allies made several successful attacks on the Ploesti Oil Refinery in Romania and other major oil refineries. This meant that we did not have to attack Ploesti, which was very well defended. The attacks also denied the Germans the fuel they needed and we always felt that the fighters were trying to save fuel. Also, there had been thousands of fighter pilots and planes shot down before we got there. So, we were on the tail end of the declining German capability to defend against bombing raids.

Bob Lick wearing an A-2 Jacket, Silk Scarf, and Parachute Harness,

---

[2] "Flak" is an abbreviation for the German word **Fl**ieger-**A**bwehr-**K**anone, meaning "aircraft-defense gun." "Ack-Ack" or "A-A" has the same meaning.

Our squadron flew every third mission and our time over there was mostly in the winter, from October to May. So, I remember that we were scheduled for a flight at the beginning of December, but we didn't actually take to the air until almost Christmas because of weather conditions.

We always knew the days we were scheduled to fly, but that schedule was subject to change at the last minute. So, when we went to bed around ten o'clock at night, we didn't know if the flight would get scrubbed before the Charge of Quarters (CQ) woke us up at 3 a.m. Or maybe we would get up and then the flight would be cancelled later.

Usually, we would go to sleep on our normal schedule and then wait for the shout when the CQ would tell us the time for breakfast and for the main briefing. We rarely went back to sleep to get a little more lay by because we were afraid of being late. We'd make sure to shave carefully so the oxygen masks would fit tightly. I seem to remember that we actually had electric shavers then. They plugged into the sockets. When we were ready, we'd go get some chow. For breakfast I usually had bacon and eggs. If it was a mission day, you'd get real eggs, otherwise they served powdered eggs in the mess hall. After breakfast we could walk to the main briefing, since Group Headquarters was within walking distance as I recall.

The briefing revealed the target location and its importance, along with any secondary targets. The route was specified and there were forecasts for enemy defenses (both flak and fighters), and for weather conditions. Emergency landing spots and Prisoner of War and escape procedures were covered. The briefing ended with a "time hack" to synchronize watches.

It could be dramatic when the target map was uncovered and we saw where we were going. Some days we exited with smiles and some days with frowns. Mostly that depended on the amount of flak expected. Munich had a lot of flak, as did the Brenner Pass. We had missions to both places. Targets in the Balkans were much favored. We only went there a few times, but those targets were not well defended so they were safe and easy. The bombardiers had a separate briefing from the rest of the crew because they had more details to cover.

We picked up our equipment after the main briefing. I would already be wearing my electrically heated flight suit and we'd get our emergency sheepskin clothes, parachute harness, mask, flak apron, etc. I never had any problems with the electric suit. It always worked fine for me.

Then we were picked up by a GI truck and taken to the flight line. We had a lot to carry. There would be two or three crews picked up together. When we arrived at the airplane, it was fully loaded with bombs and fuel. My ammo was all there and my gun was in place. We had tracers loaded with the other cartridges, probably every fifth cartridge was a tracer.

When all the planes were ready, we started taxiing when we saw a green flare. Each pilot knew his assigned place in the queue; the general order was lead planes first, then high and low squadrons in the formation. Eventually, the Group and section leading planes stopped at the head of the runway, with a bomber's length between each plane lined up behind them. A green light from the Flying Control trailer was the go-ahead for take-off. I could see these signals from my position on occasion. I was strapped to the floor with a kind of cargo strap when we took off. We didn't have seats in the back of the plane.

The lead pilot rolled first and headed down the runway. Our co-pilot set all throttles for maximum power and the flight engineer monitored instruments. A fully-loaded B-24 needed about 3,000 feet to become airborne, but we used most of the runway to gain maximum airspeed in case we lost an engine on take-off. I was in the back so I never saw these aspects firsthand.

Once in the air, our plane kept straight for about two minutes then headed to the assembly area to converge on the lead airplane, which was piloted by a fairly high ranking officer. There we took our position in the assigned squadrons. This sometimes took us as much as an hour to get together, which ate into our flight time because we were using up gas. We were "Tail End Charlie" once; the last plane in the formation. Not a good place to be since you are more vulnerable to rear attacks from fighter planes. We flew in formation all the way to the target area and then the planes would bunch up tighter for the run-in to the target.

In Formation

Bomber formations were based on the "box" concept, which arranged the attacking force into a collection of separate boxes of planes. The basic unit was a box of nine planes arranged so that planes flew spaced apart at different altitudes. No plane was directly underneath another plane. This prevented bombs from falling onto lower planes. The altitude separation helped prevent in-flight collisions and made it more difficult for the anti-aircraft gunners to shoot us down. The whole arrangement also made it possible for planes to protect each other and cover all the angles of approach when fighter planes tried to attack us. We might have 30 or more bombers gathered together for a mission, usually in two attack units. In our outfit, the standard box was nine planes, although other bomb groups might use six, as shown below.

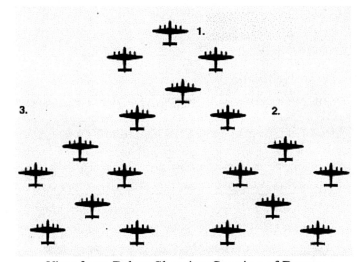

View from Below Showing Spacing of Boxes

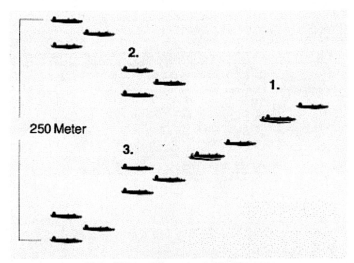

250 Meter

Side View, Showing 18 Planes
Lead Element (#1) and Trailing Elements (#2 and #3)

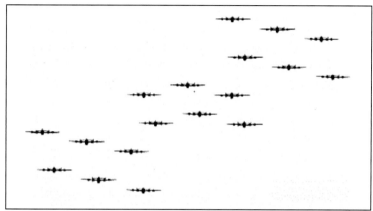

Head-on View, with Lead Element in the Middle

The bombardier, Everett Lorenz, was usually the armorer on the plane so he armed the bombs. He had to leave his position in the nose of the plane and carefully thread his way along the catwalk between the bomb bays and pull the pins to set the bombs. There wasn't room for a parachute on that walk. The Flight Engineer, John Walling, was his backup since he knew the most about the plane.

B-24s Flying in Formation

When we flew combat missions, our navigator and bombardier actually had little to do. The squadron lead aircraft took care of navigation and we followed along in formation. Routes were selected to avoid major flak areas as much as possible and to mislead enemy fighters about the intended target. Each route, then, included several course changes until the Initial Point (IP) was reached. The IP was the start of the bomb run.

The radio operator also had little to do. We all maintained radio silence when headed to the target or returning home. The only time the radios were used was when we were at the target and by then the Germans knew we were coming. It was always an operator from the squadron lead plane on the radio, giving instructions and so on. We just listened. So, I was a radio operator, but I rarely used the radio.

We sometimes encountered enemy fighters when we flew. It wasn't as bad as it was at the beginning of the war. The German jets were also starting to be used. They were scarce planes and kept their distance, certainly more than a half mile away because they wanted to avoid the .50 caliber machine gun fire. They lobbed rockets at us, but I never saw a B-24 hit by one of those rockets.

German Jet, Messerschmitt 262-A

When we headed for the target, the bombardier in the lead plane was directing the whole convoy and we dropped our bombs when the lead plane dropped theirs. So, unless there was an emergency situation, all we did was follow along and just toggle the bombs when everyone else did.

When we had to turn back from the target, we always got rid of our bombs as soon as we could because those bombs were armed and could easily be detonated. Let me ask you, would you want to be landing in a plane full of armed bombs? I don't think so.

One time, I regretted that we got rid of our bombs. We were coming back from somewhere in northern Italy, which was still under German occupation, and we jettisoned our bombs out in the open. I was charged with photographing bomb damage with an Air Corps Speed Graphic camera. I would lay my flak armor on the floor, lie down, and open up the access hatch which was just in front of the opening to the rear turret gunner's position. So, I opened the floor hatch to see what happened with our bombs, and I saw this fine farm just obliterated. Some gentleman farmer lost everything that day. I regretted that.

As we neared the target, the bombardier would often tell us to drop chaff[3] to distract the German radar. I'd drop it right through the same floor hatch in front of the rear turret.

---

[3] Strips of aluminum which create an exaggerated "return" on a radar scope to camouflage the planes.

Air Corps Speed Graphic Camera, circa 1944

We started at an Initial Point with all the other planes gathered together in formation. Then we headed straight for the target, with each plane maintaining its original heading and altitude. Our bombardier had control of the airplane's heading. We might encounter fighters when heading for the target, but they peeled off when we got within range of the flak. Then we were alone.

We didn't have a lot of head-on attacks by fighter planes, so Cleo West in the nose gunner position mainly served as a lookout for attacking planes. We couldn't see much from the waist gunners' positions, so the nose gunner, belly gunner, top turret gunner and tail gunner were our lookouts, and we'd get information from them over the intercom.

Ernie Balint, the belly turret gunner, didn't mind one bit being down there. We were rarely attacked from below, you see, most of the attacks came from above us and behind us. Ernie just shot at planes as they were leaving us and heading for home. Angelo Marino was a radio operator and waist gunner on our crew, so he and I were frequently next to each other on the plane.

In all the missions we flew, I never knew for certain that I even damaged a fighter plane attacking us. Ack-Ack (Anti-aircraft fire) was more of a problem because the .88s were plentiful and well-manned. Later in the war, our fighter planes actually started attacking anti-aircraft gun positions, but that was when the die had already been cast and the war was almost over for the Germans.

B-24, Top Turret Gunner Position

During the bombing run, planes were subject to anti-aircraft fire for about ten minutes. Oftentimes, we were shot at before we reached the IP. Most of the Germans were using 88mm anti-aircraft guns for flak fire, the best anti-aircraft gun in the world. The Germans could just fire their shells a mile ahead of us and be sure of coming close. They knew we would not be changing course and they knew what the target was and when we would be dropping our bombs.

The first sign of flak was black puffs, then the smell of black powder. Closer to the target, the red shell bursts could be seen and we heard the rainfall of small shrapnel fragments. Finally, as we neared the target, shell bursts begin to toss our plane around. It was time for good luck charms and prayers.

B-24 on a Bomb Run

After we dropped our bombs, we just lit out for home. We didn't rally all the planes and then fly back in formation. We said when we were headed for the target that we were "Flying for Uncle Sam" and followed orders, but on the way home we were flying for ourselves and acted in our own best interests.

When we landed and taxied to our parking spot, we were greeted by Medics as soon as we exited the plane. They asked us if we were OK and made sure we hadn't been injured. Then they gave us our medicine – two full shots of bourbon. I always carried an empty bottle on the flight and when somebody on our plane or other returning planes said, "I don't want this much bourbon," I'd pour it into my bottle and save it for later.

After a mission, I would turn over my camera to the intelligence department. I don't think I ever took the film out of the camera; just turned it over to them and then they'd use the film to make assessments of bomb damage. Unfortunately, I never kept a notebook to make a record of each mission. The closest I have is a mission log I picked up somewhere which closely mirrors the missions we flew in the same time period. I'm not sure who created that log, but the missions are similar so it must have been someone in our squadron. [See Appendix.]

B-24 over Wiener – Neustadt Industrial Area

450th Bomb Group B-24 in Flight, Open Bomb Bay doors and Waist Gunners Portal

We also had a debriefing after every mission. We'd review the whole mission and the Intelligence Office would record everything that happened and pass the information to the higher echelons of the Air Corps.

Debriefing

Our flight engineer wrote a short account of one of our missions. We didn't know it at the time, but that place had been bombed the day before and a couple of B-24s were shot down. The Intelligence Officer's report on this mission is in the Appendix.

December 17, 1944, Wels Austria Marshalling Yards

By John R. Walling, Flight Engineer
William A. Donald Crew

Most screwed up mission ever. Clouds from ground level to us. Came out of clouds and bomb group nowhere to be seen.

Started flying north. Hooked up with another B-24 group. Flew until tanks ½ empty. Peeled off, dropped bombs, and headed south.

Found out later group got hit by fighters about 10 minutes after we left. Flying south alone, no fighters. Started following B-17 group flying about 10,000 feet. Nose gunner told Lefkowits (the Navigator), "B-17s made slight right turn."

Pilot had gone to bomb bay to use relief tube. Navigator said, "Wait a minute I about got us located." Nose gunner (Leo West) said, "Lefty, there's a town up ahead on this river. (Gyor, Hungary)."

Then all hell started. Heavy flak all around plane. Smoke up through the bomb bay. Pilot (W.A. Donald) returning to flight deck jumped in seat and put plane in dive and zigzagged. Radio Operator (Angelo Marino) on flight deck looked at me as if to say, 'What do I do now?' and I thought 'Beats hell out of me.'

We lost #4 engine and were losing oil in #2. Heading to Manduria I was off intercom watching engines and transferring gas. Found out later the crew was getting ready to ditch in the Adriatic.

Finally got back to Manduria, ground crew was waiting. Good to see them.

Write up on mission said one plane experienced some flak. Really lucky to get back after all the chances to go down.

Pilot later visited a B-17 pilot who was telling him about the B-24 they saw go down. Asking about the time and date, he told the B-17 pilot, "That was my plane." The B-17 pilot did not believe him, said, "No way that plane could have survived."

A TURRET GUNNERS LIFE

S/Sgt Harvey S. Rusco, 722nd Squadron

A guy comes in and wakes you up;
What's coming you may dread.
You're wishing it was raining,
So you could stay in bed.

You go over to the Mess Hall
To get a little chow,
And the coffee that they give you
Will wake you up right now!

You go back to your barracks,
Hang your mess kit on the wall;
Grab up the old flying bag
And stagger down the hall.

You go and draw a flak suit,
And lay it on your bag
All this time you're praying,
Your bomb load isn't "frags."

You head then for the Briefing Room;
No one knows what's on your mind.
The reason you couldn't sleep at night
Was because of a small red line.

It could have been Ploesti;
No rougher could exist.
The boys behind those flak guns
Very seldom ever missed.

No, it's not Ploesti,
Because that line of red
Isn't going in there at all;
It's going north instead.

No, it isn't Budapest;
It gets a little higher.
That line of red heads no place else
Than right straight up to Steyr.

We're briefed on several hundred guns
And fighters by the score.
Your chin drops down upon your chest
As you shuffle out the door.

You get up on a G.I. truck
That takes you to your plane.
You pray to God that before too long,
You can ride that truck again.

You check your turret in and out,
And shine the plexiglass.
To prepare for all the fighters
That are apt to make a pass.

The crew loads up, the engines roar,
With the ground crew standing by.
They pray you'll make a safe return
As they wave their fond "good-bye."

The pilot runs the engines up.
We move down the taxi-ways,
And wait our turn to go;
Here the whole crew prays.

We move out on the runway;
The engines cough and whine.
The pilot moves a foot or two
To make sure we're in line.

The pilot then takes off the brakes;
We're off to see the town.
At eight fifteen the stick comes back,
Now we're off the ground.

We circle the field an hour or more,
And then we're off "on course."
I clear my throat and try to talk,
But I see I'm a little hoarse.

At 12,000 feet we all are dressed;
Now comes on "the mask."
We're set now for the job to come-
It may be quite a task.

We fly for hours--we're stiff and cold,
By now our eyes are sore
From looking for the flying hell
That we've seen so much before.

Now we hear a mike switch click
And know it's going to be,
"Navigator to the crew,
We're now on our 'I.P.'."

We all get set with flak suits;
The old chute close at hand.
A second look for fighters,
And then a glance at land.

You pull yourself into a ball;
Your feet don't feel so bad.
A cold sweat hits your face;
Your heart is running mad.

The nose gunner hits his mike switch;
His voice comes to the back,
"We must be here, just look ahead,
The sky is full of flak."

You wait for just a minute;
It seems an hour or more.
Then you hear that "barking" sound,
One we have heard before.

You're asking God to see you through,
For that you really pray.
Then you hear those joyous words;
Just two, they're "Bombs Away."

The pilot rocks her sideways,
To miss a load of flak.
You're feeling pretty good now,
More sure of getting back.

About that time, you see a speck,
Then a couple more.
Holy gosh, it's fighters, and
They're coming by the score.

Time to turn on turret power
And to holler to the crew.
The escort better show up soon
Or we're apt to not get through.

You're breathing hard & thinking fast;
A second more will tell.
Then you'll get them or they'll get you;
That second's really hell.

Another flock of fighters,
P-fifty-ones and thirty-eights.
They were hiding, just awaiting,
And using us for bait.

The Huns peel off and try to run,
But they're a little late.
Half are meat for fifty-ones,
The rest for thirty-eights.

You tell someone to pinch you
To see if you are dead.
You know that mission's added
Some gray hairs to your head.

We land back at the home base;
We now feel pretty good.
We got back on that G.I. truck,
Just as we prayed we would.

Before you see your barracks,
Your mind begins to roam;
And you're thinking of the letters,
That you should get from home.

You realize you're back again;
How good terra firma feels.
Now you thank the Lord again,
For you're sure of three more meals.

B-24 Gunner on a Carpet of .50 Calibre Cartridges

CHAPTER SIX -- Life at the Air Base, Manduria, Italy

We were on an airbase which had previously been used by the Italians. Of course, we upgraded the runway because we needed concrete, not gravel. That was all done before I got there. A lot of the buildings were put up by the base personnel, including the mess halls, hospital, etc. Chow on the base was pretty good. Just let me say, I didn't complain about it.

I was really only on leave once, the rest of the time we had nothing scheduled so we'd simply leave the base and go sightseeing. Passes weren't tightly controlled in our area. We generally flew every third mission. So, once we flew a mission, we figured we'd have at least two days off.

We'd hitchhike up to Taranto. Lefty and I often went up there to walk around and take in the sights. He and I had a lot in common, with our college backgrounds. I also went on trips with John Walling the Engineer and with the tail gunner, Vern Miller. Sometimes when I try to recall what happened back then, I have a hard time separating what I knew then and what I knew later. I ask myself was that when I was a Sergeant, or was that when I was a human being?

Taranto, Italy, The River Bridge.

Ocean Concourse, Taranto, Italy

That one time I was on leave, we decided to head west to the toe of Italy; Manduria was on the heel. We probably went about 20 or 30 miles away to the coast where they still have a lot of antique watchtowers. We decided to climb a tower on the outside, and I did OK until I got stuck. I lost touch with the steps and I couldn't go up or down. Fortunately, there were 10 or 15 Yugoslavians in the area and those guys gathered underneath me, so that in case I fell they could cushion my fall. They remained in place for about ten minutes until I finally located a ledge I could step onto and then make my way to the ground.

Watchtower in Southern Italy, circa 16th Century

When we were on base, we were sleeping in a ten-man tent with a pyramidal roof, just six of the enlisted members of the crew. We were in a sea of tents. Winter was coming on when we arrived, so we hired a local stone mason to build six foot side walls. He was satisfied to be paid with a carton of cigarettes.

The tent then acted as the roof mostly. The canvas was arranged so that that the rain drained outside the walls. We had a comfortable place to stay then. We had a metal stove and the winters were not really severe in southern Italy.

Our tent was well away from the action on base, so we didn't get a chance to see many movies or USO shows. I wasn't ever much interested in movies anyway. We could go into town, which was a much better deal than the guys who were stationed in Africa and confined to base. We hitchhiked when we wanted to get places. There was a lot of Army traffic and they'd stop if they had extra room.

Angelo Marino's parents were from Rome and he spoke Italian well enough for people to recognize that he had a Roman accent and vocabulary. When we'd go looking for someplace to eat, the natives would recognize that Angelo had that connection with Rome. The food wasn't very good at that time due to the shortages all over Italy. I remember being invited to someone's home for dinner and we never returned because the food wasn't too good. The same thing happened in restaurants we found when out sightseeing.

Bob Lick, Manduria, c. 1944, Crew Tent at Left, Chow Hall in Rear is Officer's Mess

Bob at the Mess Hall Stirring Up Trouble

Ernie Balint Headed for Chow

My Dad was also in Europe at about the same time, also working for the Army. He volunteered before the war even broke out. He got in touch with the Army in 1937 and said he'd be willing to serve if they needed any help. He had moved up the ranks with the Frisco Line and was an executive then. The Army said, "Sure, we'll let you know but you will have to pass the physical exam." Then about every six months they'd send him a telegram asking if he was still willing to serve and Dad always said "Yes."

After D-Day when the allied troops were advancing across Europe, the Army finally needed Dad's help. Without warning he was notified to report for indefinite duty in Washington, D.C. So, he packed up and got on the train. He arrived on a Wednesday, passed his physical and was sworn in the next day as a Lieutenant Colonel and put on a plane to London. He was only two days in the U.S. He arrived in London on Friday. They put him on a plane to Paris the next day. So there he was in Paris running troop trains for the U.S. Army. He'd never had a bit of Army training.

Joseph Franklin Lick, c. 1940

I first heard about Dad's new job when I got a letter at Manduria with a return address of "Lt. Col. J.F Lick, Army Post Office 887" or something. He was telling me that he was in Paris, so we tried to get together, but I was still flying and the Army had better things to do than send me to Paris.

Dad was in the Army for about two years total. He continued to serve for a while after the war was over. He was quite a conscientious man, so I expect he did a good job running trains and he was certainly qualified for the job. He told me that he had a Russian Countess who worked as his translator. It wasn't all bad. Dad was in his 40s then and was being paid as a Lieutenant Colonel.

In one instance, some General (I like to think it was Patton) had the bright idea to give his troops some Rest and Relaxation at some French coastal resort before they were shipped out to the Pacific. His request for a troop train was denied, so the General simply commandeered a train and sent his troops to their R&R. Of course, Dad was quickly notified by the French railroad authorities and recovered the train right away. I suppose the troops were trucked to their final destination.

Hospital Train, European Theatre of Operations, c. 1944

CHAPTER SEVEN -- After the War

After we finished 51 missions, we departed Italy on May 5, 1945, right before the war ended, leaving from the port of Ostia just downriver from Rome. While we were crossing the Atlantic, we heard that the Germans finally surrendered and Victory in Europe had been declared. We were the first troop ship to land in Boston after V.E. Day. That was on May 15, 1945.

Just a few years ago I visited the same ship. I'd look around and remember my wartime experiences, such as the place where the gamblers gathered. There was a lot of gambling on the ship, shooting dice and so forth. I stayed well away from that. We had friendlier games at Manduria, but on that ship there were high stakes.

The first and only time I was ever assigned to kitchen duty (Kitchen Police or KP) was on the ship headed back to the states. The lowest ranking soldiers got that duty, and by that time in the war the lowest ranking guys on that ship were Tech Sergeants just like me. All the other places I'd been, I was good friends with the company clerks and they kept me off the KP rosters. Sometimes I was even in charge of making up those rosters. But on that ship, I got assigned and there was no way out of it.

The Army kept shuffling me around after I arrived in Boston. I don't know why. Maybe they thought I'd be needed in the Pacific. It took me almost six months to finally be released. I was often volunteering in the office as a typist then, and I could decide what my orders would be and write them myself. My buddies would cover for me if necessary. I remember playing golf in Reno a lot when I was assigned to an air base out there, and I also worked for Railway Express for a while until I got further orders. Eventually I was discharged on October 17, 1945, at Scott Field in Rantoul, Illinois. My total longevity for pay purposes was 2 years, 10 months, and 22 days. My total time overseas was 7 months and 28 days.

I picked up a few decorations and citations in that time period. I already mentioned qualifying with the M-1 Carbine. I also received six bronze stars which were affixed to the Europe Africa Middle East Theatre ribbon, known in the Army as the EAMET ribbon. Anybody who was assigned to that part of the world picked up that ribbon. Bronze stars were awarded to air crew members based on the number of missions flown. I suppose that since I flew 51 missions, I received six bronze stars.

Six Bronze Stars on an EAMET ribbon

I must have received three air medals because I have the Air Medal with two oak leaf clusters attached. Oak leaf clusters are used to indicate that you won the medal again. Air Medals were awarded to aircrew members who completed a certain number of missions; I'm not sure how many.

Air Medal with Two Oak Leaf Clusters

I was also authorized a good conduct ribbon and one overseas bar along with the lapel pin, which is for an honorable discharge. They called that medal "The Ruptured Duck."

Lapel Pin

My military specialty in the Air Corps was #757, a Radio Operator, Mechanic Gunner.

Because we had missions all over the place, the Army recorded me as participating in the following battles and campaigns:

- Rome-Arno
- Northern Apennines
- Po Valley
- Rhineland
- Central Europe
- Air Combat Balkans

Colonel Joe Lick, Helen Lick, and T/Sgt. Bob Lick

After the war, I decided to go to a bigger university rather than return to Drury College. I really didn't feel that I had a home anymore in Missouri. I thought about Indiana University, Northwestern in Chicago, and Ohio State, finally selecting Ohio State. I majored in Marketing there. That's where I met my wife, Dorothy. I was in Lambda Chi and she was a Phi Mu. We were married in 1948 on June 12th.

Bob at Ohio State University, c. 1946

Dorothy and Bob on Their Wedding Day, June 12, 1948

By 1950, Dorothy and I were living in Marion, Ohio and I was working for the Marion Shovel Company as an advertising man.[4] I was then 27 and she was 22. We lived at 178 St. James Street in Marion. Dorothy was working as a demonstrator of electrical appliances for a utility company. She switched her major to Home Economics as soon as we were engaged, so she was the right person for this job. Our son, Jeff, was born that year.

Marion Power Shovel at the Hanna Coal Mine

---

[4] The Marion Steam Shovel Company built the primary tools for America's civil engineering projects for more than 100 years. Founded in 1884 by Henry M. Barnhart, George W. King, and Edward Huber, the company's patented steam shovels helped revolutionize railway and road construction, and were used in the building of the Panama Canal, Hoover Dam, and the Holland Tunnel. "The Shovel" also built ditchers, log loaders, dredges, and draglines, including some of the largest land vehicles ever built. The first electric machine was built in 1915, but it was not until 1946 that the name was changed to Marion Power Shovel. In the mid-twentieth century, "The Shovel" employed 2,500 workers. In the 1960s, the National Aeronautics and Space Administration selected Marion to build the crawlers that transport spacecraft to their launch pads. Hundred-year rival Bucyrus International acquired and closed the company in 1997.

Marion Power Shovel Watch Fob

The Marion Steam Shovel Co., Bird's Eye View. Depot in Center Foreground

I met a fellow named Bill Dunning at Marion Shovel. Dunning also served with the Army, protecting the U.S./Canadian border from a Japanese invasion. When I met Bill, we had an apartment that had a shared bath with another apartment, and we suggested to Bill that he live in that second apartment since we were good friends at work. He became my best friend.

After working for "The Shovel" for a few years we wound up in Cleveland. Dorothy's family was from Cleveland, so we were there every weekend for dinner. In Cleveland, I began my career with MacLean-Hunter Publishing Company out of Toronto. MacLeans had a lineup of 36 trade publications and I sold advertising in "Coal Mining & Processing" and "Rock Products." This magazine work took me throughout Ohio, Pennsylvania, West Virginia, and New York, calling on companies in the heavy mining and construction industry. I must have driven more than a million miles in my lifetime. When CB radios were popular, I talked with truck drivers, using the name "Space Man" since that's what I did — sold space in magazines.

MacLean-Hunter Toronto Office, 1946

In 1980, I was promoted to Publisher in the Chicago office and Dorothy and I moved to Barrington, Illinois. We had three more children well before that. Wendy was born in 1953, Lisa in 1954, and Laura in 1960, so they were all finished up with high school by then (at least). After the three older kids were grown, Dorothy taught pre-school.

When we moved to Barrington, we decided to buy an ultra-modern house, which was designed by Harry Weese, a well-known Chicago architect. The house was first built in 1952 and had slate floors, an open plan interior and lots of windows in the back.

111 Hillside Avenue, Barrington, Illinois

I commuted to work downtown and was able to grow our business, while acquiring a few of the competitive publications.

In those years I don't think I ever got on a plane without Dorothy. We traveled together to trade shows all over the U.S., Canada, and the rest of the world. She was essential; helping me entertain clients, staffing the display booth and maintaining friendly relations with everyone we met. She knew everybody.

I retired in 1991 and Dorothy and I had 25 more years together before she passed away in 2016.

Bob and Dorothy After Retirement

I should mention that I also helped to organize some small reunions for the crew. I was most compatible with the Navigator and Flight Engineer, "Lefty" Lefkowits and John Walling. I kept in contact with them after the war was over.

Lefty and I organized a couple reunions. The first one was pretty successful; a lot of the crew attended. The Co-Pilot, Allen Smith, wasn't there; we never found out what he did after the war. We lost track of him before we even left Italy. Perhaps he stayed with the Air Corps.

Our pilot did show up, William Donald. Unfortunately, that was the last time we saw him. He may have felt uncomfortable because our relationships had changed. He was working as a shoe salesman at the time. I had finished college and had a good job. Quite a different outcome in our lives. Lefty also was doing well.

He and I talked about what we could do to attract William Donald back to our reunions, but we were never successful.

I want to add that I decided to take an Ancestry.com test in 2020, and they said I'm from all over northern Europe, more specifically:

- 41% England and NW Europe
- 23% Scotland
- 21% Ireland
- 9% Sweden
- 6% Germanic Europe

Ancestry said that it seems likely that sometime in the 18th century my ancestors migrated from northwest Europe to the Carolinas, Maryland, or Virginia, which would have put them in the colonies prior to the American revolution. I created a family tree on ancestry.com which includes 960 people and dates back to 1753, so that's consistent with Ancestry's story.

I believe both my mother's family (the Conners) and my father's family settled in the Carolinas. There are Licks in that area; and their heritage is preserved in some old homes. One was built by Martin Lick, a carpenter, in 1787 at 512 Salt Street. It's one of the very earliest standing log houses in Forsyth County. A subsequent owner, Johann Leinbach, a shoemaker, bought the house in 1795. He traded extensively in salt, thus giving the street its name. To add to its fame, a poet named John Henry Boner was born there in 1845. This house was restored in 1952. The other house on that street is the **Matthew Lick house at 512 Salt Street**, which was built in 1822.

In the 19th Century, many of these early settlers made their way directly west to the southern portion of the midwestern states. This may explain why some people think I'm a southern gentleman, and also explains how the Conners and Licks found their way to Missouri.

Matthew Lick House, 512 Salt Street, Winston-Salem, NC

Laura Mandell, Solomon Lick House, 524 Salt Street, Winston-Salem, NC

Appendix

The B-24 Liberator, by Richard O'Hara

450th Bomb Group, December, 1944 Narrative

A mission log acquired by Bob Lick

Intelligence Office Report
December 17, 1944
Raid on Wels, Austria, Marshalling Yard

The B-24 Liberator
By Rich O'Hara

In January, 1939, the Army Air Corps invited Consolidated Aircraft Company to submit a design study for a bomber with longer range, higher speed, and greater ceiling than the Boeing B-17 Flying Fortress. A contract was awarded in March, and Consolidated finished the prototype and had it ready for its first flight two days before the end of 1939.

The plane featured a highly efficient wing, which helped the plane meet the Army's requirements. This was a plane focused on long-distance missions carrying large bomb loads. However, the B-24 was relatively difficult to fly and had poor low-speed performance; it also could not fly as high and was less reliable than the B-17 bomber.

The B-24 was used extensively in World War II where it served in every branch of the American armed forces, as well as several Allied air forces and navies. It saw use all over the world. For much of 1944, the B-24 was the predominant bomber of U.S. Strategic Air Forces in the Combined Bomber Offensive against Germany, forming nearly half of its heavy bomber strength prior to August and most of the Italian-based force. Thousands of B-24s dropped hundreds of thousands of tons of high explosive and incendiary bombs on German military and industrial targets.

Consolidated Aircraft Company Patch

The new high lift wing was combined with the twin tail design of Consolidated's flying boat along with a new fuselage encasing two bomb bays, each being the same capacity of the B-17 bomb bays. In total, the plane could carry 16,000 pounds of bombs, with half on each side. The bomb bays were traversed by a centerline catwalk just nine inches wide, which also functioned as the fuselage's structural keel beam.

An unusual set of all-metal, tambour-panel "roller-type" bomb bay doors, operated very much like the movable enclosure of a rolltop desk, and retracted into the fuselage. When opened up, these created a minimum of aerodynamic drag which helped keep speeds high over the target area, while also allowing the bomb bays to be opened while on the ground since the low ground clearance would otherwise prevent the use of normal bomb bay doors.

B-24 Fresh from the Factory

The wing allowed a relatively high airspeed and long range, but became unpleasant to fly with heavier loadings. It was also more susceptible to ice formation than other designs, causing distortions of the airfoil section and resulting in the loss of lift, with unpleasant experiences drawing such comments as, "The wing won't hold enough ice to chill your drink." The wing was also more susceptible to damage than the B-17's wing, making the aircraft less able to absorb battle damage.

The plane was powered by four supercharged Pratt & Whitney Wasp R-180 radial engines which turned 3-bladed variable-pitch propellers. The tailplane featured two large oval vertical stabilizers mounted at the ends of a rectangular horizontal stabilizer.

The B-24 featured a tricycle undercarriage, the first American bomber to do so, with the main gear extending out of the wing on long strut legs. Because it had no nose wheel steering, the pilots used differential braking and differential thrust for ground steering, which made taxiing difficult.

Camouflaged B-24 under Tow

At approximately 18,500 units -- including 8,685 manufactured by Ford Motor Company alone -- it is the world's most produced bomber, heavy bomber, multi-engine aircraft, and American military aircraft in history. Multiple airplane types were designed and built (mainly A to J), each one with some new improvements.

Crew Members and Positions

The Liberator carried a crew of up to ten. The pilot and co-pilot sat alongside each other in the upper cockpit. The navigator and bombardier sat in the lower nose, which also held two flexible ball-mounts for forward defensive firepower using twin machine guns operated by the nose gunner. The radio/radar operator sat behind the pilots, facing sideways and sometimes doubled as a waist gunner. The flight engineer sat adjacent to the radio operator behind the pilots. He operated the upper gun turret, located just behind the cockpit and in front of the wing.

Up to four crew members could be located in the waist, operating waist guns, a retractable lower ball turret gun, and a tail gun turret matching the nose turret. The waist gun hatches were provided with large doors. The ball turret was required to be retractable for ground clearance when preparing to land as well as for greater aerodynamic efficiency. The tail gunner's powered twin-gun turret was located at the end of the tail, behind the tailplane.

Tail Gunner Position

Flying the B-24

It was said that you could spot a Liberator pilot by his over-developed left arm, from muscling the control yoke. The plane did not accept being flown out of trim, hands off, and you couldn't easily find the right trim setting. The airplane itself did not perform well at all without all four engines. Combat tended to increase the risk of losing an engine, another problem that added to its poor reputation.

B-24 Cockpit

In Fate Is the Hunter by Ernest K. Gann he unreels a litany of complaints about the B-24:

"It was a ground loving bitch, and with heavy loads it rolled, snorted and porpoised interminably before asserting its questionable right to fly. The failure of any one of the four engines on takeoff was an extremely serious affair. The flight controls were heavy and insensitive, compared to other airplanes. This was particularly true at lower altitudes.

No one knew how best to winterize the plane, which created a continuous series of minor crises. Landing gears would not go down when activated, and sometimes they would not retract. On one occasion, we flew about for hours with one wheel up and one wheel down. This ludicrous, stork-like attitude canceled the pauper's choice of a decent belly landing.

The propeller pitch was controlled electrically. At least once during the flight the mechanism was bound to freeze, which left us helpless to reduce speed properly, or climb out of adverse weather. The transfer of fuel from the reserve tanks to the operational tanks was necessary on a flight of any duration. It was a nervous and odoriferous business. All smoking was stopped, while the smell of high octane gasoline marinated the entire airplane. We stopped smoking because the connecting hoses invariably leaked, some enough to make troublesome puddles on the floor. A high octane wading pool is something you can't throw out the window.

Throughout this eye-burning transfer process, we also kept the radios silent, with the idea of preventing explosion. It never seemed to trouble any of us that the fuel transfer pump was also electric, and gaily throwing out sparks within a few feet of the hose connections.

No heat was provided in the plane. It was always cold at operating altitudes -- minus 40° or lower. To prepared to fly, first we put on our regular long-john underwear, then electrically-heated blue long underwear, and heated shoes. Over the electric underwear went the flying suit. This was a dark green "Ike" jacket and matching pants. We plugged into a socket located at our crew positions. Next, we put on heavy fur-lined boots, and, of course, we had fur-lined gloves. As if this wasn't enough to immobilize us, we also wore or carried a "Mae West" life preserver (to inflate in the event we ditched at sea), a parachute harness, an escape kit, and other items. Believe it or not, we got along pretty well with this apparel. But frankly, it was a hell of a nuisance if one had to urinate, and even worse, God forbid, if one got the "GIs" while on a mission!

B-24 Waist Gunners Loading Ammo Belts

Strange as it seems, no separate entryway into the aircraft was provided. Crew entered and exited through the bomb bay. There was so little clearance under the parked aircraft that crew had to squat, bend and slide under the airplane, stand up in the open bomb bay, get up onto the narrow catwalk and crawl into position. Considering the clothing and gear each wore or carried, that wasn't easy to do. Upon return from a long hard mission, it was even more difficult to exit that way.

It was difficult, sometimes impossible, to exit the plane when ordered to bail out. In some nose turret models, the bombardier could not exit the turret until one of two turret closures were opened by other crew. It was clearly miraculous that so many crewmen did parachute from stricken planes, given the weight of their gear, the inconvenient or inaccessible exits, and the centrifugal forces holding the flyer pinned to the wall as the aircraft spun, rolled, or tumbled out of control.

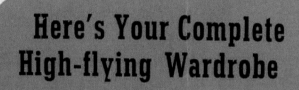

Here's Your Complete High-flying Wardrobe

1. Jacket
2. Jacket Insert, Heated
3. Trouser
4. Trouser Insert, Heated
5. Helmet
6. Shoes, Felt
7. Shoe Insert, Heated
8. Glove, Heated
9. Rayon Glove Inserts
10. A-12 Mittens
11. Scarf
12. Lead Cord
13. Woolen Shirt
14. Light Socks
15. Long Underwear

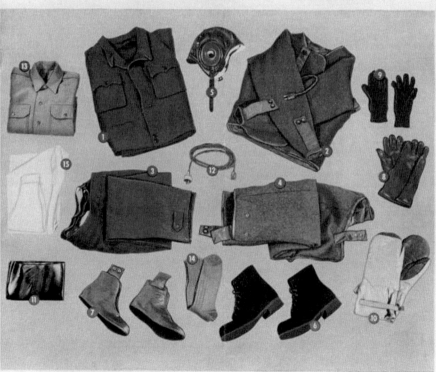

THE electrically heated suit assembly is designed to maintain top body efficiency of the wearer during routine flight, training or combat flying for all temperature conditions to 40 degrees F. below zero regardless of the time duration of flight.

Poster, c. 1943, High Altitude Clothing

Another B-24 pilot, Lt. Don Jones related a number of stories of his experiences. In their overseas movement from the U.S. to the U.K., Jones flew the B-24 aircraft on the long southern route. He said, "The southern route was fairly uneventful, but one thing I recall -- our 8½ hour flight across the South Atlantic Ocean from Brazil to West Africa was on instruments. The auto-pilot was out so I had to hand-fly that turkey. The B-24 was notoriously hard to fly; it took lots of muscle to move it about."

Jones, speaking of the reasons B-24 bombers were lost, told of one unexplained case. He said,

"Every once in a while, but rarely, we would just be flying along at high altitude, going on or returning from a mission, with no flak and no fighter opposition, and one of our B-24s would just blow up! There never seemed to be an explanation for such a disaster. I worried a lot about it. Our fuel tanks were located in the wings. I thought maybe gasoline or fumes were escaping. That happened in our airplane. You would smell fuel in the bomb bay. Now the main hydraulic pump for the entire airplane was located on the right-hand side of the bomb bay and it was pressure-activated--that is, if the pressure in the hydraulic system went down a little bit, it would switch the pump on automatically. At the altitude we were flying I thought it could arc. With arcing and a heavy concentration of fuel fumes, you would have a big firecracker on your hands. As a safety measure, I would roll the bomb bay doors open every half hour or so and flush out the fuel vapors. I felt this was a worthwhile safety measure. Well, anyway, we never blew up! This may have helped."

Fully-equipped Waist Gunner

Flying Combat Missions

According to one estimate, there were 20 personnel in a supporting role on the ground for every bomber crew member in the air. The remainder of this essay touches on the roles played by various air corps support personnel and the crews they supported.

The Air Corps heavy bomber force in Europe was organized into two main air forces, the 8th Air Force handled England and northern Europe. The 15 Air Force was responsible for the Mediterranean and southern Europe. The 15th AF was composed of several bombardment wings, including the 47th wing, which was based at Manduria, Italy. The wing had four groups, including the 450th Bombardment Group, the "Cottontails." That group had several squadrons, including the 722nd Bomb Squadron, which was the unit which counted Bob Lick among its members.

There were substantial numbers of coordinated activities among these different organizations. The chief focus was putting a crew in place to put bombs on target, but a host of supporting functions helped make that happen.

The strategic targeting decisions started at the 15th Air Force level, selecting suitable targets from a prioritized list, which primarily included railroad marshalling yards and oil refineries in 1944/1945. The enemy made the same calculations, hoping to predict when and where the Allies would bomb strategic targets. The Americans nearly always flew daylight bombing raids and their planes took off near dawn, so predicting what time in the afternoon a target might be hit was relatively easy. Targets with clear skies were especially alert for raids.

Blechhammer Oil Refinery, Germany, August, 1944

Field Orders detailing each bombing raid were passed down the chain of command. Wings and Groups started their mission preparations. Base services were notified, including the Commanding Office, the operations office, intelligence office, Group Navigator and Bombardier, Weather Office, ordnance and armament sections, engineering office, signals and photographic units, mess hall, transportation, and the Charge of Quarters (CQ, or duty sergeant) on each squadron living site. A list of available planes and crews was created and assignments made. Crews were finally told when they would be flying

In the War Room, the Intelligence officer decoded the target name, plotted the target on aerial photos while clerks assembled maps, photos and all other target material needed to brief combat airmen. Operations personnel affixed a ribbon to the large map in the briefing room to show the route to and from the target and points of fighter escort (if any).

Working backward, planners needed to allow at least an hour from the first take off for formation assembly (longer if the weather was poor); 10-15 minutes for marshalling and taxiing; 10-15 minutes for starting engines; 10 minutes for crews to board aircraft; an hour before engine start for crews to inspect their plane; an hour for main briefings; an hour for breakfast; and 30 minutes for crews to be awakened. Reveille for combat crews was therefore about 5 hours before take-off time.

The Ordnance Section was informed as soon as the required bomb load was learned and bombs moved onto trailers at the bomb dump, transported to the aircraft parking spots, and loaded into the planes. Other personnel brought belts of .50 calibre ammunition to the planes. The machine guns, removed from the planes after every mission for cleaning, were also brought back.

The bombs had a fuse in both the nose and tail; as a precaution, these were inserted at the last minute. A cotter pin kept the firing pin locked in place, preventing detonation.

Delivering Bombs

Ordinance teams usually loaded the bombs using muscle power. One man would hoist the front of the bomb, one would hoist the back end, and a third would squat so the middle of the bomb rested on his back. Then they would lift up together.

Aircraft maintenance personnel were awakened about three hours before take-off. The crew chief and assistant crew chief pre-flighted their plane. They began by manually turning each propeller to remove fuel in the cylinders and circulate the oil. Then the crew chief climbed into the cockpit and began engine priming procedures. After starting a portable generator to boost battery power, the assistant, with fire extinguisher at hand, positioned himself near the engine to be started where he could also see hand signs from the cockpit. The first engine cranked up was always the one that drove the plane's electrical generators.

The main briefing was attended by everyone in the selected crews. The "highlight" was when the mission map was revealed. The route in and out was shown by a thin line of red tape pinned on the map. It was covered with a cloth that was drawn aside as the mission briefing commenced. As each briefing ended, the men went to the personal equipment room and collected their flying equipment. Escape kits with foreign money, maps, matches, chocolate, and other items useful in evasion were distributed. When properly equipped, the airmen were taken to their planes.

Dropping a Load of Small Fragmentation Bombs

Returning back to base, the flight engineer confirmed the wheels were down and locked. Planes with wounded aboard fired two red flares landed first, turned off the runway as soon as possible, and halted on the taxiway or where the ambulance was waiting.

Trucks took the men to the briefing room, which was now set up for interrogation. Every crew was checked in by an Intelligence Office clerk who verified each man's name and position. Any changes from the original crew load lists were reported on a "Sortie Record" to ensure that everyone got credit for completing the mission.

Aircrews first reported "hot news"-details on convoys, aircraft in distress, etc.-that needed to be transmitted right away. Crews were then thoroughly questioned. Using a preprinted Interrogation Form, the debriefing officer noted crew comments about their bombing attack; personnel injuries and plane damage; equipment malfunctions or failures; enemy encounters; friendly fighter support; and locations and types of flak encountered.

Their responses were compiled. Navigators turned in their logs and bombardiers completed bombing reports. Lead crew command pilots, navigators, and bombardiers wrote detailed accounts about what they did and why. Finally, crews were released to go to the mess hall or to their barracks.

HEADQUARTERS 450TH BOMBARDMENT GROUP (H) AAF
APO-520   US ARMY

S-2 [Intelligence Office} NARRATIVE REPORT
MISSION DATE: DECEMBER 17, 1944

MISSION NBR. 195

TARGET: Wels, Austria - Marshalling Yard

I. CHRONOLOGY

At 0814-0838 hours, thirty-six B-24 type aircraft took off to bomb rolling stock in main marshalling year at Wels, Austria. Two aircraft returned early, having lost formation in heavy cloud mass in north Adriatic. Thirty-two aircraft dropped 66.25 tons of 500 lb. RDX[5] bombs on the target at 1211 hours from 19,000 - 21,500 feet. Three leaflet bombs were also dropped on the target.

Five aircraft jettisoned 12.5 tons five miles beyond the I.P. when leader's accidental release caused four other bombardiers to Toggle prematurely. One other jettisoned 2.5 tons 30 miles NNE Vienna. This aircraft had lost the Group formation in the clouds over North Adriatic and attached himself to a B-24 formation headed north. Upon discovering that the formation was attacking a target some distance north of Vienna the decision was made to return with a B-17 unit moving south. Bombs were jettisoned through solid undercast and no attempt made to hit a specific target.[6]

One early return jettisoned 1 long delay bomb and 3 others (1 ton), in Adriatic at 1050 hours. 1.5 tons were returned to base. The second early return jettisoned 3 bombs, (.75 tons) in the Adriatic. 1.25 tons were returned to base. One bomb (.25 tons) was jettisoned due to hang-up. One aircraft is missing and is not believed to have gone over the target. Disposition of bomb load of this aircraft is not known. Thirty-two aircraft returned at 1530 hours. One other returned 1645 hours. One is missing.

II. ROUTE AND ASSAULT

The 450th Group (Wing Lead) rendezvoused with 449th Group over Manduria at 0905 hours on course to San Vito. The briefed route was flown to I.P. and the target attacked on an axis of 60 degrees True Course. A sharp right rally was executed to avoid flak at Linz and Steyr, thence on briefed route to base. The attack was made by attack units of two 9-ship boxes each. The I.P. was closed in with sold undercast and the run was made by synchronous PFF method.[7] The bombs of the lead ship of the second attack unit were dropped prematurely near the I.P. due to an electrical

---

[5] RDX stands for Royal Demolition explosive whose chemical name is 1,3,5-trinitro-1,3,5-triazine. It is a white powder and is very explosive.

[6] The William Donald crew.

[7] "Blind Bombing" using the primitive radar available at the time.

malfunction but the leader continued on over the target. A synchronous PFF run was made and the bombs dropped on the leader's signal in lieu of the usual practice of toggling on his bombs-away.

Thirty-six P-38's contacted the formation at Millstatter Lake at 1140 hours at 20,000 feet and provided penetration, target and withdrawal cover to Sansego where they departed at 1345 hours. 9/10 strata-cumulus, tops at 10,000 feet prevailed over the Adriatic, clearing over Pola. The Alps were fairly clear except for haze in the valley. From Millstatter Lake to the I.P. about 7/10 scattered cumulus was experienced. This thickened at the I.P. and 10/10 solid undercast, tops 10,000 feet formed over the valley leading into the target and extended to the south for 20 miles. Villach was clear on return. Condition in Adriatic were similar to route out.

III. RESULTS

No visual results were possible due to solid undercast. No terrain features were visible in the photos. The lead "Mickey" operator picked up the I.P. clearly and turned in towards Linz on heading of 60 degrees True Course.8 The target was clearly identified 25 miles out and good Bombardier-Mickey coordination was reported. Bombs are believed to be in the target area and very likely hits were scored on the marshalling yard.

IV. ENEMY RESISTANCE

A. Fighters: None.

B. Flak: 25-30 bursts were observed to the left rear after rally. If directed toward formation they were obviously short on range and low. It is believed guns were located at Horsching, 8 miles to the NE.

V. OBSERVATIONS

At 1241 hours from 18,000 feet near Saak (46.35N-13.37E), a B-24 was seen to slip down through the clouds and level off very low going between canyons in the mountains just left of the town, on a heading 198 degrees.9 One engine was trailing white smoke when last seen at 1250 hours.

What was believed to be a destroyer was observed in harbor at 45.00N-14.05E at 1109 hours from 17,000 feet.

At 1143 hours from 19,000 feet the marshalling yard at Spittal was observed to be heavily loaded with cars. Approximate number was not reported.

---

8 The "Mickey" was the radar set used in selected planes.
9 Heading south for home when last seen.

VI. CONCLUSION

A. Losses: One aircraft missing. Lost formation and indicated intention to bomb target of opportunity and return to base at approximately 1130 hours.

B. Damage: Aircraft #954 which went north of Vienna with another group formation ran into flak at Gyor on return and received slight damage.10

C. Casualties: None.

D. Victories: None.

Wels Marshalling Yard, Bomb Damage Assessment, Date Unknown

---

[10] Likely another reference to the William Donald plane. Plane #954 was called "Marge."

STEADFAST!

Historical Record - December 1944

450th BOMBARDMENT GROUP (Heavy)
NARRATIVE DECEMBER 1944

"Forward March!" The 450th was on its way to the ramp on the first of December, 1944 to witness a presentation of awards to members of the organization who had been wounded in action or who had achieved distinction at their post. One could hardly expect propitious weather in Winter at the heel of the Italian boot, so the tramp of soldiers was more like a slosh, slip, splash of two thousand feet trying to keep in step through the soft mud of mid-winter. The icy breezes blowing from the Gulf of Taranto had nothing of that exotic thrill ascribed to them by romantic writers who extol the balmy scenes of "Sunny Italy." To officers and men standing at attention with bespattered shoes and wet feet, the bucolic milieu of mud, olive groves and bleak weather literally stunk!

Twelve months in Manduria had taught all to build and dress for the weather, and Uncle Sam had provided the materials with which to make this possible. A year ago the camp was a quagmire accentuated by the dearth of supplies caused by the sinking [of supply ships] at Bari by the German Stukas. Today, we take stock proudly of Mess Halls, Day Rooms, and Operation Buildings built with Tuffi [soft volcanic rock] and roofed with American tar paper or corrugated iron. And as for quarters – everything from a concrete floored tent to a California Mission Bungalow with hot and cold running water.

Italian Tuffi Mason

Assistant Masons

Life overseas is now a definitely established routine. A year ago the first Liberator broke through the undercast, circled the field and came in for a landing. In it was Colonel John S. Mills, Commanding Officer of the 450th. Today planes are serviced, missions are flown, meals are served, men come and go, all this in all kinds of weather, and at any time decreed by higher Headquarters. Is the 450th in a rut? Hell no; they are housebroken. When the war ends – oh well, nobody thinks about it anymore. What's the bomb load today?

ACTIVITIES:

No longer will audiences run for cover when the downpour starts – and just when Dorothy Lamour was about to shed her sarong. The new indoor "Cottontail Theater" was opened on December 3 with a concert by Madame Eustis. Nine hundred bomb stools were occupied by as many men, with a couple of hundred more standing along the walls. They could not believe their eyes when they saw a full sized stage, screen, powerful lights, projection booth and all. It was quite a treat to sit indoors where the body heat of a thousand hot-blooded soldiers took the chill air out of the room. Major Jackson of S-4 [logistics coordination] need not lose any more sleep. The Italian structural steel held up, and the corrugated iron did the trick for walls and roofing. Now bring on all the stage shows and movies.

The S-2 Building addition is ready for the roof. Major Harwood, Group S-2 Officer, is reading the Book of Job in order to bear up under the stress of building, and is about to go broke buying materials which will reach him through channels sometime after the armistice. "It all started when I mentioned a ten by twelve office, and then someone threw in a yeast cake. Now look at that overgrown hangar!"

The Ari Base Group Aid Station, known in ordinary parlance as the "Hospital" is running a neck to neck race with the weather, but the Italian masons keep chipping away at their Tuffi and the Flight Surgeon keeps calling for "Ancora" and "Subito! Subito! Get the lead out of your Pantalone!" It seems to work, for the first wing is already roofed and the ground is broken for the next one.

The Group Officer's Mess Hall was getting too crowded with all the additional personnel in Headquarters, so there was only one thing to do: enlarge! Here was a job for the spanking new Second Lt. Kuhn, erstwhile top-kick of the 722nd Squadron. A week later we moved into a large "Dining Room" with tables for four, new dome lights, freshly painted walls, and white table cloths. All this and napkins too. Now that "Gino" the Italian Club Caretaker has been elevated to Head Waiter by Mess Officer Captain Wells, (Group Adjutant) eggs will be eggs instead of "ekkis," and "hotti Kekkis" will revert to hot cakes. And who ever heard of "zuppa" for cereal?

The extension of the runway, for-you-know-what, (or do you?) is crowding the 723rd Squadron out of its area, so the order is Move! Sgt Toliver and Captain Olman thought they had enough headaches, but now they'll take aspirin instead of atabrine. [antimalarial pills] The Doughty Top-Kick [First Sergeant, the highest ranking enlisted man] shoved his cap over his right eye, spat out some terbacker juice and barked: "Did you ever see a squadron move from scratch? I'll have that 723rd across the road so quick it'll make your goddam head swim – beggin' yer pardon, sir!"

With a theater, a radio station, a weekly newspaper and basketball team, the next thing was a band. Yes, the 450th is going collegiate! Special Services promises us a Drum-Majorette also, but since it is not OEL equipment we may have to take "Eyetie" issue. Anyhow, a call had been put out for musicians and several have been uncovered. There's Lt. Cylkowski with his Julliard Conservatory Moniker, and then, too, a certain Lt. Eisler whose Father wielded the Metro Baton in New York for 20 years. There is a band in the offing, sure 'nuff.

And in case anyone thinks that our college hi-jinks is all hoopla, they should step into our class rooms and see everything from calculus to languages and counterpoint being taught. "Cottontail University" is in full swing in December. The latest addition to the faculty has occupied the Chair of Physics. He is Captain "Robby" Robinson, of Yale, already well known in ping-pong circles where the Chaplain is ready to take all comers, and I mean "take."

Close on the heels of Lt. Kuhn's promotion came S/Sgt. Hollingsworth's Field Commission as a Gunnery Officer. He was old enough to accept a commission, but too young to enter Gunnery School. Captain Stevens, 720th C.O. was up at the Fifth Army Front getting a bit of Front Line color when the orders came through changing his bars into Gold Leaf. He did not seem to be a bit attached to his "railroad tracks."

When four Line Chiefs were sent to a special school in Bari, there were many whispers and much speculation. Those in the know had it right from the horse's mouth that they were being trained for B-29 maintenance. It was a Military Secret, but it had leaked out. The Line Chiefs came back bursting with knowledge about the care of B-24 tires!

In addition to the regular weekly news lectures, the S-2 Section has instituted a 15 minute news flash account in the War Room every day at 11:45 for all Dept Heads and Commanding Officers. With the excellent map facilities in the War Room there is no excuse for not knowing the latest in World War News. This feature has been received with much enthusiasm.

If you can't make the show at 1800 Wednesday, shall we say, you can meet your buddy on the ground floor at 2000 and see the second show. But should you be tied up with such social obligations as KP or Guard Duty, you can wait and catch the Matinee on the following day. Not only that, but you can be choosy and look over the menu for the week and make your own selections. If you are in a frivolous mood, you'll go on Mondays; if you want a nice news lecture before the Piece De Resistance, you'll choose Tuesday; if it's a five star reel you are dying to see, Friday is the day;

but if you want a stage show with girls, girls, girls in the flesh, you'll save all your lip smacking until Saturday night. Sunday morning at 10 AM you may go back piously and cleanse your wicked soul, for on the day the chaplain holds services.

During December the Cottontail Theater billed a no small number of attractions outside of its regular share of first and third rate shows. On December 3, there was Madame Eustis whose trills are known to American audiences. She made her style GI and tried to sing what the boys like to hear.

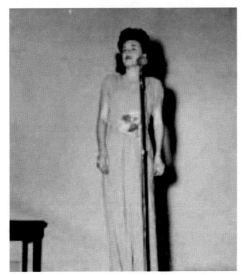

Singer

Lady Accordionist

On December 16th the "Broadway Varieties" did a good job of entertaining the Cottontail audience with the "Dizzy Ditties Deftly Done" by Owen and Parker and the Ventriloquacious, Miss Carole whose "Tommy" got nicely rough at times. The "Magician" had the usual card trick routine that is supposed to make audiences go ga-ga, but to which GI's well conversant with cards respond courteously. The inevitable lady accordionist who played badly and sang worse was also there -

Ho hum!

The Ping Pong artists on December 28th went through a few antics deftly performed but that is as far as the show went. The treat of the season, however, was the excellent production of "Rhapsody in Blue" based on the life of George Gershwin. Knowing that they were being treated to a World Premiere presented at their brand new Cottontail Theater, the 450th behaved with all the dignity and decorum befitting the occasion. The three hour show went through in great style. The power did not break down. The new film held and the sound track was as clear as could be wished for. (Hold your breath, for there are a few guys who insist on smoking in the theater despite the prohibiting signs).

MORALE:

Nothing like piles of mail to boost morale in the Theater, and no month like December to bring in letters, Xmas greetings and parcels. Despite the enormous quantities of mail sacks that Sgt. Herman had to sort he was able to keep his temper at an even keel. Mail was his business before he joined the Army so it's only been a change of station for him.

The resumption of the trips to Rome has brought back the gleam to the GI's eyes. They are thinking of the interesting historical sites they will soon visit, and then too, travel is so broadening.

No morale can stay up without a few rumors to hold it up. "Parlor" gossip has been busy dishing out a few "have-you-heards" in December. Foremost among these are the facts that the 450th will be converted to B-29's, or was it B-32's? And if you don't believe it, look at the recent extensions of the runway. We also have it from those in the know that the Distinguished Unit Citation will be presented to us in January; that a Rest Camp is being opened in Southern France with young Mademoiselles as waitresses and everything. "OU LA LA! MAIS OUI. TOUJOURS L'AMOUR."

OPERATIONS:

The increasingly poor flying weather in December cut down our missions to nineteen, most of which were carried out by PFF. However, on the eight instances in which visual bombing was possible, the boys did an excellent job. With the exception of four trips to refineries in Southern Germany, and Austria, all bombing was concentrated on the enemy's communications. With the gradual knocking out of the Axis' Satellites, the 450th have been greatly reduced. The overall bombing percentage for December put the 450th in the lead with a score of 67.1%

VITAL STATISTICS:

The Strength at the beginning of the month was only 2,388 but by the end it had jumped to 2,517. Nineteen missions were flown during the month with a total of 473 sorties, 66 of which were ineffective. There were 0 officers and men MIA and one KIA. With the cooperation of Marshall Tito in Yugoslavia, a large proportion of these crews parachuting from damaged bombers will be safely returned to their base. Captain Vincent Taylor, young Commander of the 723rd Squadron was hit in the head by a flak fragment and died at the controls of his plane as he was leading an attack against the Brenner Pass on the 29th.

AWARDS AND DECORATIONS:

There were a few more decorations pinned this month than the proceeding one, but the Bronze Star is still playing "hard-to-get." The following figures tell the story:

- Silver Star   1
- Distinguished Flying Cross   35
- Bronze Star   1
- Air Medal   172
- Oak Leaf Cluster Air Medal   245
- Purple Hearts   16
- Good Conduct Medals   121

CHRISTMAS SPECIAL ACCOUNT:

Four days after arriving in Manduria, Italy, Christmas came to a group of bewildered members of the 450th Air Echelon. They sat on their assorted gear, in the dark foul-smelling wooden barracks recently vacated by what once had been the "Reggia Aeronautica Italiana." Most of the conversation on that Xmas evening of 1943 centered around the subject of the next Christmas. Tired of travel, mad, rain and exposure, the men pulled on their flying clothes and lay down to wait for Santa Claus – that was 1943.

Preparations for Christmas began early in December of 1944. The 721st Squadron posted a $100 prize for the best trimmed Xmas tree, and that sent every GI hurrying to "downtown Manduria" to look for tinsel, artificial snow, and Christmas Decorations. The Italian merchants, already accustomed to demands for stores they never heard of, simply shrugged their shoulders, grinned, and answered in a gradual crescendo of "NON C'E, NON C'E," meaning "we ain't got it." Someone going into the olive grove (not for purposes of worship) happened to see a few strands of Window [a.k.a. Chaff] hanging from the olive trees. That was the answer! Next day when the judges passed on the best tree in the 721st Area they could not decide whether Sgt. Pietz's tree was better than Pfc. Gaeta's so they split honors both ways and awarded them $50 apiece. There was plenty of "tinsel" for decoration.

Down from the "Forests" of [censored] came truckloads of Christmas trees which were distributed among those who planned to have a tree "at home."

The Day Rooms, Officer's Clubs and even Mess Halls were decorated in Yuletide Spirit. Squadrons vied with each other in an effort to create the real Christmas atmosphere, and despite the lack of snow just then to make it a White Xmas, they succeeded in creating the illusion of a Homey Christmas.

For the preceding two months the boys had combed Bari, Lecce and the surrounding towns for souvenirs and suitable presents to send home. There was an increased traffic in such items as cameos, jewelry and ready to wear. Everywhere, the Italian street merchant tried to entice with signs and pleadings: "VERRA GOODA CAMEO, NAPKEENS, TEBLE CLOS – HANDA MADE."

The Army Gift Shop in Bari proved a boon to the soldier with money in his pocket. The assurance that they were getting their money's worth loosened the purse strings of the wary. Connoisseur of cameos insisted on the more expensive products from Torre Del Greco personally turned out by the able artisan "Salvatore," all from $35 and up (paid advertisement)

But no American Christmas would be complete without there being some giving as well as receiving. And, since every American soldier is considered wealthy in Italy, it was expected that he should pass out a few bon-bons to celebrate the advent of one whose prime mission was to give. The orphanage of Oria had provided a concert at camp with a choir of 100 boys and a 20 piece orchestra. They sang Christmas Carols for two hours in the theater and broadcast over the "Voice of the Cottontails." We listened to the music but could not recognize any of the so called carols until the choir struck "Silent Night." The program ended with the rendering of the familiar "Adeste Fideles." The PX ration candy that had been donated beforehand was distributed amongst the orphaned boys who from the alacrity with which they went at it must have had a first class Christmas belly ache the next day.

Yugoslav Orphan Gifts

Those who had bailed out over Yugoslavia and had tasted of Yugoslavian Hospitality were foremost in contributing to the Yugoslav Orphans. All manner of candy, cookie sand sundry items were deposited in boxes at the PX's as the officers and men drew their rations. The chaplain, assisted by Escapees from Yugoslavia, packed the donations, and sent them on their way to Tito's Boys.

For Protestants there was a service at 10 am and also one at midnight at the theater. The Catholic Churches in the surrounding villages afforded ample opportunity to those who wished to attend services. Some fortunate visitors to Rome attended Mass at St Pete's along with 150,000 others. The Protestant congregation in Oria had their Christmas Program at 3 pm. A good number of American soldiers and officers including Chaplain Keefe and Chaplain Mayfield of the 62nd Service Group were present. They too received their share of candy and gifts from the 450th. Urchins on the street, hearing that candy was being distributed to the Protestant Congregation ran in declaring that they too were "Protestante."

The Colonel had overhauled the interior of his Italian storehouse and added a few of the embellishments that make American life enjoyable. There was a large open fireplace, electric lights, comfortable furniture, and rugs on the floor. Add to all this the Christmas Decorations, a tree, and stockings over the hearth and you have a scene as American as corn on the cob. In the midst of these surroundings, Colonel Jacoby played host to his staff on Christmas Day preparatory to the sumptuous dinner that was to follow. The olives, crackers, fruitcake, and other goodies he had received from home went into the Cocktail Party as "Aperitif." Those who needed a drink (this hot, dry climate) found one already mixed – eggnogs, mind you."

The Colonel's Bash

Visiting Dignitaries

Put a good drink in a man's hand, a cocktail table before him filled with olives, fruitcake and stuff, and a warm fireplace behind him, and he'll forget he's in Italy. We all forgot that for a moment. Anyhow, the "Old Man's" reception was a big success - - but gosh! Christmas is so long in coming!

Mission Log Acquired by Bob Lick

Depar-ture Time	Date	Target	Mission Credit	Total	Crew	Ship	Results and Remarks
540	10-Oct-44	Northern Italy	1	1	Chubb & Crew	285	Target OVCST [overcast]; returned with bombs [Target was Padua marshalling yards (M/Y)]
530	11-Oct-44	Vienna	1	2	Stine & Crew	285	Target OVCST; returned with bombs. [Targets were two oil refineries near Vienna.]
630	13-Oct-44	Banhida, Hungary	1	3	Own	789	Fairly good bombing. [Target was M/Y.]
705	16-Oct-44	Wiener Neustadt, Austria	2	5	Own	789	Lousy; things all screwed up. Worked from flight deck for first time, OVCST, returned with bombs. [Target was St. Valentin Tank Works.]
650	23-Oct-44	Brenner Pass	1	6	Own	928	First time; OVCST, returned with bombs. [Target was rail line at Brenner Pass.]
845	4-Nov-44	Munich M/Y	2	8	Own	928	PFF bombing,* landed Bari Foggia [for gas].
720	6-Nov-44	Vienna	2	10	Own	928	PFF bombing, Moosbier oil refinery [near Vienna].
725	7-Nov-44	Brenner Pass	1	11	Own	954	Very poor, messup by deputy leader, and we dropped on him,** 3 runs on target
800	16-Nov-44	Munich	2	13	Own	458	PFF, very poor log, results of bombing not known yet.
805	17-Nov-44	Vienna	2	15	Stine + mixture	285	PFF on Floridsdorf oil refinery, landed Foggia for gas, Stine finished up with visual with 40/100 pounders, easy, short and sweet.
630	18-Nov-44	Aviano airfield, (north Italy)	1	16	Own	928	[Successful, but no notes.]
400	21-Nov-44	Doboj R.R. Bridge in Yugoslavia	1	17	Own	596	Got near target but weather no good, so brought bombs back.
520	23-Nov-44	Zenica R.R. Bridge in Yugoslavia	1	18	Own	954	Good job, bridge finito
	26-Nov-44						35 Sortie Deal becomes official
700	6-Dec-44	Sopron Marshalling Yards, Hungary	2	20	Own	928	Bombs on target, lost box, joined strange group, went terrific flak at Gyor - [returned] alone.
815	17-Dec-44	Wels, Austria marshalling yard	2	22	Own	954	Up well past Wien, came back alone
710	20-Dec-44	Salzburg Austria M/Y	2	24	Own	954	PFF, results unknown, very poor, #1 messed up.
	24-Dec-44						News came that they are being counted both ways.

Depar-ture Time	Date	Target	Mission Credit	Total	Crew	Ship	Results and Remarks
705	26-Dec-44	Ora R.R. Bridge, loop in R.R.	1	25	Seiple	804	George and I flew deputy, no flak at target, heavy and accurate
715	29-Dec-44	Brenner Pass	1	26	Own (As NB) ***	894	At Brenner 1st time as toggler, PFF, close and moderate flak.
750	15-Jan-45	Vienna, S.E. M/Y	2	28	Own	918	At target, oxygen trouble. No log. Weather near ? at 25,000' Lousy. Salvoed .5 [tons of bombs] in Adriatic [to reduce load and enable plane to stay in formation.]
715	1-Feb-45	Vienna Moosbierbaum	1	29	Own	954	Came back. Feathered #3. ****
720	15-Feb-45	Vienna	2	31	Own	804	PFF - [Flak] close & heavy & intense. I dropped bombs. [Target was Matzleindorfs M/Y.]
740	21-Feb-45	Vienna	2	33	Hall + crew	804	Visual - flak damn close. Target-lousy, weather SQL [squalls.] Came back alone.
745	22-Feb-45	Rosenheim M/Y	2	35	Own	387	Bombs NMTTS [?]. Scant, accurate flak at 2 places.
158	25-Feb-45	Linz M/Y	2	37	Own (as NB)	387	Heavy and accurate flak. #4 hit. Came home alone with it feathered.
700	1-Mar-45	Vienna, Moosbierbaum Oil Refinery [O/R]	2	39	Own	954	PFF. Not much flak.
745	8-Mar-45	Kamarom M/Y	2	41	Own (as NB)	918	Primary [target] UNDCST. Went to Maribor [Locomotive Depot] Alt [altimeter] malfunction in #1 ship. [remainder obscure]
720	12-Mar-45	Florisdorf M/Y Vienna.	2	42	Own (as NB)	524	PFF, flak pretty close at times. [Original target was the Florisdorf oil refinery.]
745	13-Mar-45	Regensburg M/Y	2	45	Own (as NB)	789	PFF, no flak
700	16-Mar-45	Wienerneustadt M/Y	2	47	Own (as NB)	927	Visual, no results, no flak
800	19-Mar-45	Landshut M/Y	2	49	Davenport (NB)	804	Visual -hits-no flak.
705	20-Mar-45	Amstetten M/Y	2	51	Vandermere	863	Visual-short-no flak. [Secondary target was hit. Primary was St. Valentin Tank Works]

FINITO!!!!!!!

* PFF-bombing was also called blind bombing. A pathfinder plane equipped with an H2X air-to-ground radar would identify the ground target and drop skymarker smoke parachutes over the target. The radar was not very accurate, however, and skymarkers would drift.

** "Dropped on him" means that Link's plane dropped their bombs at the same time as the leading plane since they couldn't spot the target on their own.

*** "As NB" means as Navigator/Bombardier.

**** "Feathered #3" means that they turned the prop on #3 engine so that it stopped providing propulsion, usually done when the engine was malfunctioning.

STEADFAST!

Fifty-one Missions in a B-24 Liberator

By Robert J. Lick

Consolidated
Publishing

Oviedo, Lucca, Nara, Boise

Also Available from Rich O'Hara

===

Home from the War; Ten Accounts of World War II

Drawn from War; The Sketches of Sergeant Victor A. Lundy

Streator Boys, Three Veterans of World War II

The Pacific War and the Peace That Followed.
Conversations with Roald B. Forseth

Streator Air Service; An Illustrated and Annotated Episodic History

John Charles Frémont's Adventures

- *Volume I, From Savannah to the Racoon River*

- *Volume II, Across the Plains to the Wind River Range*

- *Volume III, From the Missouri River to Fort Vancouver (1843)*

- *Volume IV, To Alta California and the Great Basin*

- *Volume V, The Turning Point*

The Narrow Roads; In Search of Old Japan

The Trail to Tenri City; The Old Road South of Nara

Precious Stones; the Poetry Monuments of the Yamanobe no Michi

The Sisters of Mercy; Remembering Our Days at St. Mary's.

The Glass Bottle Manufacturing Capital of the World,
Some Stories from Streator, Ill.

America's Greatest Minstrel, Honey Boy Evans

The Sensation of the Century; Streator's World-Famous Zouaves

Little Star, the Story of Vaudeville from Beginning to End

About the Editor

Richard O'Hara is a prolific writer whose previous books include *Home from the War; Ten Accounts of World War II* and *Honey Boy Evans, America's Greatest Minstrel*. The book you're holding in your hands is his sixty eighth publication.

He grew up in Streator, Illinois, learning to bait a hook at an early age and roaming the banks of the Vermilion River with his pals and his faithful dog, Spot. Rich read voraciously in the shade of an old elm tree, and was the darling of the local librarians.

As an undergraduate at the University of Illinois, he was included in President Nixon's first draft lottery in 1969 and his number was 9. By the time his college deferment expired, he had enlisted in the U.S. Air Force, and reported for duty on December 21, 1971 at Lackland Air Force Base in Texas. He completed navigator training at Mather field and Castle air base in California, and was assigned to a KC-135 aerial refueling plane in the Strategic Air Command. He flew combat in 1974 in Indo-China while on temporary assignment from the 904th Aerial Refueling Squadron. Rich left the service in the fall of 1977 as a Captain.

He's now retired after a 30-year career in the environmental field and lives in Boise, Idaho, with his wife, Patti, an actress and artist of note.

Rich O'Hara, Official Portrait, c. 1976

Made in the USA
Monee, IL
03 December 2024

72242276R00055